Introduction

Goods and livestock have been transported across the length and breadth of the country in motor vehicles since the latter years of the nineteenth and the early formative years of the twentieth centuries.

Road hauliers were in competition with the railways to transport goods, especially from the 1930s through to the 1960s, when the railways were in their heyday. But once Dr Beeching had cut many railway lines in the 1960s, the upper hand fell to the road hauliers and they went from strength to strength, which is visibly noticeable by observing the number of lorries and vans seen on Britain's roads in the present day.

The definition of commercial vehicles can vary. For example, the European Union definition covers any vehicle that is built and designed to carry more than nine people including the driver (therefore buses, coaches and minibuses come under the commercial vehicles category). In the United States of America a vehicle is regarded as a commercial when it is titled or registered to an officially recognised company (which can also strangely include company cars).

There are many varied types of vehicle that are classified as commercial vehicles, ranging from articulated lorries to small panel vans, and also include recovery/breakdown trucks – bizarrely hearses also fall into that category. All have the same thing in common: they are all financially beneficial to both operating companies/individual and customers alike. The vehicles that I shall be featuring within the pages of this book will be a varied plethora of different manufacturers, many of which are well-known household names while some not so well-known ones are thrown into the mix as well.

1. The Beginning

Before any commercial vehicle can begin making their owners or customers any money, they have to be manufactured. These vehicles all begin life as a metal chassis, upon which the vehicle is built up from and around. This chapter looks at a few of those chassis, some of which are derelict and awaiting either restoration or eventual scrapping.

Founded in 1895 in Guildford, Surrey, Dennis Brothers Ltd specialised mainly in the manufacture of buses, fire engines and lorries. All of their vehicles were made to order for the customers' requirements, which resulted in them being stronger built than mass-produced vehicles. On 16 September 2016 during a pre-auction viewing at the Blackborough House, near Kentisbeare in Devon, this 1930 30cwt lorry chassis was seen.

In 1904 Harry Underdown and Horatio Hutchinson founded Commercial Cars Ltd in order to produce commercial vehicles, fire engines, omnibuses and other industrial vehicles. The trading name applied to their vehicles was 'Commer'.

This 1954 chassis may not be much to look at as it awaits its turn at auction in Elmstone Hardwicke on 24 August 2012, but strangely enough it was in a structurally sound condition and therefore made it an ideal candidate for anybody willing to make a restoration project out of it.

Gary, Indiana, during 1916 saw the founding of The Gary Motor Truck Company, who built lorries ranging from 0.75 to 2 ton capacities. In 1922 the company became Gary Truck Corporation and a wider range of trucks ranging between 1 and 5 ton capacities was manufactured. The company lasted for five more years but finally went out of business and closed in 1927.

Built in *c.* 1920 and noted at the 12 September 2015 Statfold Barn Railway Enthusiasts Day, this is the chassis (and front end) of one of the companies' 1-ton models.

In 1921 Harry Shelvoke & James Drewry left the Lacre Motor Company and went into business as Shelvoke & Drewry, based in Letchworth, Hertfordshire. The most successful vehicle in their range was the Freighter, which was the basis and forerunner for the first multi production in municipal vehicles. This 1930 chassis was seen at a pre-auction farm dispersal sale viewing in Elmstone Hardwicke, Gloucestershire, on 24 August 2012.

New Year's Day in 1924 saw a new commercial vehicle manufacturing company formed, when William Morris (founder of Morris Motors Ltd), founded Morris Commercial Cars Ltd. These vehicles were branded as 'Morris' and 'Morris-Commercial' and would remain so until 1968 when they were incorporated into the British Leyland Motor Corporation.

A farm dispersal auction at Elmstone Hardwicke on 24 August 2012 had this *c.* 1940s-built tipper chassis from a Morris Saurer as one of the lots. Note the wooden 'tipper' sub-section part and the hydraulic vertical pole, along which the body moves in order to elevate it to the tipping position.

In April 1931, Vauxhall Motors decided to enter into the commercial vehicle market, and did so under the name of Bedford Vehicles, which proved to be a profitable and successful venture lasting for over fifty-five years, before being acquired by General Motors.

This unidentified chassis was built by the company in the 1950s and was seen at Elmstone Hardwicke on 24 August 2012, note the various farming equipment – waiting to be auctioned off the following day.

COMMERCIAL VEHICLES BUILT BEFORE 1960

ROYSTON MORRIS

AMBERLEY

First published 2022

Amberley Publishing
The Hill, Stroud
Gloucestershire, GL5 4EP

www.amberley-books.com

Copyright © Royston Morris, 2022

The right of Royston Morris to be identified as the Author of this work has been asserted in accordance with the Copyrights, Designs and Patents Act 1988.

ISBN 978 1 3981 0504 1 (print)
ISBN 978 1 3981 0505 8 (ebook)

All rights reserved. No part of this book may be reprinted or reproduced or utilised in any form or by any electronic, mechanical or other means, now known or hereafter invented, including photocopying and recording, or in any information storage or retrieval system, without the permission in writing from the Publishers.

British Library Cataloguing in Publication Data.
A catalogue record for this book is available from the British Library.

Origination by Amberley Publishing.
Printed in the UK.

With the closure of the automobile and motorcycle manufacturers A. J. Stevens & Co. Ltd (A.J.S) in 1931, the five brothers, Harry, George, Joe, Jack and Billie, set up a new company under the name Stevens Brothers (Wolverhampton) Ltd in May 1932. This new company would concentrate on designing and developing a three-wheeled light commercial van.

Noted during a Black Country Vehicle Manufacturers' show on 29 July 2012 at the Black Country Museum in Dudley, West Midlands was this 1932 example, which only consisted of the chassis and front forks and is a restoration project for its owner. Note the cardboard 'cut-out' front wheel.

2. Powered by Steam

A few of the more well-known names of commercial vehicle manufacturers began in the late 1800s/early 1900s, building and repairing steam wagons. These were the earliest types of powered commercial vehicle after the horse-drawn wagon. Household names such as Atkinson, Foden and Sentinel all built these types of vehicles before moving on to making petrol and later diesel varieties.

1842 saw the founding of an engineering company in Lincoln by brothers-in-law Nathaniel Clayton & Joseph Shuttleworth, who would primarily concentrate on the manufacturing of portable steam engines. The name of Clayton & Shuttleworth Ltd would eventually become one of the biggest in steam vehicle production.

FE 3344 is a 1920-built Clayton & Shuttleworth wagon (works number 48510), which was a furniture removal vehicle. It was noted on 16 September 2012 taking part in the Great Henham Steam Rally held at Henham Park in Suffolk.

In 1856 a Sandbach-based agricultural equipment manufacturing company, Plant & Hancock, took on one Edwin Foden as an apprentice. Five years later, shortly after his twentieth birthday, he became a partner in the company. In 1887 George Hancock retired and the company was renamed to Edwin Foden, Sons & Co. Ltd and they started manufacturing steam-powered lorries.

Pictured at the Great Dorset Steam Fair on 5 September 2009 is this 1928-built six-wheeled Asphalt carrying steam wagon (works number 13008). Note the unusual rear twin-axled double wheels complete with solid rubber tyres.

Foden works number 13316 was built in 1929 as a steam-powered tanker. On 5 September 2009 it was taking part in the annual Great Dorset Steam Fair (carrying Joseph Dovey & New Forest Cider decals). Note how the spoked wheels by this time had been replaced and the tyres are the more traditional rubber pneumatic type.

1894 saw James Mann & Sidney Charlesworth set up an engineering business in Leeds, manufacturing a variety of steam-powered vehicles as Mann & Charlesworth. In 1899 Charlesworth left the firm to pursue a new venture, and the company was reorganised as Mann's Patent Steam Cart & Wagon Company.

Pictured on a sunny 12 July 2009 at the Hollycombe Steam and Woodland Garden Society in Liphook, Hampshire, works number 1120 was built by the company in 1916.

At the turn of the twentieth century, in 1901, a new company emerged in Leeds, West Yorkshire, by the name of the Yorkshire Patent Steam Wagon Co. In 1911 the company changed name and became Yorkshire Commercial Motor Co., but reverted back to its original name eleven years later in 1922. The company ceased production of steam vehicles in 1937 and was finally dissolved in 1993.

Noted under an ominous-looking sky at the Somerset Steam Spectacular in Low Ham on 19 July 2009, works number 2108 was manufactured by the company as a dropsided vehicle in 1927.

In 1907 brothers Edward & Henry-Birch Atkinson founded Atkinson & Co. as manufacturers and steam wagon repair specialists. They lasted for sixty-three years until the company merged with Seddon Diesel Vehicles Ltd of Oldham, becoming Seddon-Atkinson Vehicles Ltd.

One of the few surviving of their steam wagons is this 1918-built example (works number 72), which was noted at the Preston Steam Services 2005 Steam Rally and Country Fair on 26 June.

In 1813 brothers Robert and William Tasker founded the Waterloo Ironworks near Andover. Two of Williams' sons took over the company in 1857 and an agreement was made with Clayton & Shuttleworth to service and sell their stationary engines. The company was liquidated in 1903; however, Williams' third son Henry managed to secure financial backing and the company was reformed in 1907 as Tasker & Sons, and business thrived producing steam rollers and 'The Little Giant', which became their bestselling light steam engine (over 300 of which were built). After the First World War there was an economic slump and the company went into receivership and liquidation in 1926. Not to be beaten, Henry and his sons revised the company in 1932 under the name of Taskers of Andover (1932) Ltd and they would continue until the 1980s when they were taken over by Craven Industries Ltd.

This tipper wagon was built by the company in 1924 as works number 1915. It was noted at the Milestones Living Museum, Basingstoke, on 1 March 2014.

Mechanical engineering company Alley & Maclellan, formed in 1875 in Polmadie, Glasgow, manufactured valves and compressors for steam engines before moving onto steamship building. In the early years of the twentieth century they began producing road steam wagons and during 1915 they moved the production of these vehicles to a new site in Shrewsbury under a new company known as Sentinel Wagon Works Ltd.

The 5-ton Sentinel Standard wagon were the first type built, and were similar in appearance to the wagons that were being produced by Atkinson at the time. This example was one of those and was pictured on 6 May 2013 at the Abbey Hill Steam Rally in Yeovil: works number 3899, which was built in 1921.

The most popular and numerous type built by the company were the DG and Super-Sentinel series vehicles, which were introduced following the end of the First World War. The heavy overcast sky looms ominously above this 1928-built DG4 type (works number 7651) during the Great Dorset Steam Fair at Tarrant Hinton on 5 September 2009. The number after the DG denotes the number of wheels on the vehicle.

Works number 8351 is a DG6 type that was built at Shrewsbury in 1930 and was pictured on 30 December 2007 at Preston Steam Services near Canterbury. Note the works plate situated on the side of the cab (there is another one on the other side). Also note how the two back wheels are coupled together; this is because they are chain driven underneath.

The Somerset Steam Spectacular held at Low Ham, near Langport, on 19 July 2009 saw works number 9032, which is a 1934-built S4 type wagon (the company's second bestseller), complete with trailer – this was an extra that was supplied by the company if it was required by the customer.

3. Three-Wheeled Vehicles

A couple of companies that were involved in the manufacture of motorcycles branched out using motorbike technology and produced three-wheeler lightweight vans for commercial use. Also other manufacturers specialised in three-wheeled vehicles for commercial use.

Founded at Long Acre (near Covent Garden) in 1902 as the L'Acre Motor Car Company, who built a small range of cars and lightweight 2.5-ton vans. By 1909 they had become the Lacre Motor Company and they began building lorries with a 9-ton capacity – the most well-known types being municipal road sweepers. In 1928 the company found itself in trouble and the factory was sold and wound up. However, a new restructured company known as Lacre Lorries Ltd was formed in 1930 and they would last for another fifty years before final closure came in 1980.

Pictured on 21 August 2009 at the Chetwynd Deer Park in Newport, Shropshire, at the Tern Valley Rally was this 1936-built road sweeper.

This 1938 example of a former Borough of Great Yarmouth Corporation roadsweeper was taken on 12 August 2007 at the East Anglian Transport Museum, Carlton Colville in Suffolk.

After years of service with the Manchester Corporation Cleansing Department this 1948 Lacre-built roadsweeper enjoys its retirement from service as it is preserved and on display inside the Greater Manchester Museum of Transport, where it was pictured on 26 January 2013.

In 1904 mechanical engineer Herbert Clayton and his son Reginald formed Clayton & Company in Huddersfield, West Yorkshire, where they would build municipal and light commercial vehicles under the brand name of Karrier. Following the First World War in 1920 the company was renamed Karrier Motors Ltd, to separate the motoring and non-motoring sides of the business. They were acquired by the Rootes Group in 1934. The Karrier brand was used until the early 1970s – ironically the mechanical and electrical engineering side of the original company remained active at least until 2018 as Clayton & Co. Penistone.

In 1929 the company started producing The Colt, a three-wheeled refuge collection wagon, which was further developed a year later, becoming The Cob, which was produced exclusively for the London, Midland & Scottish Railway to haul their fleet of road trailers. Pictured at the National Railway Museum in York on 17 July 2012 was this 1931-built example.

In 1837 a wheelwrights and coach building company, G. Scammell & Nephew Ltd, was founded. The dawn of the new century and the following years were hugely successful and saw the company expand from twenty-two employees to over 170 by the outbreak of the First World War. Lt Col Alfred Scammell was injured in the war and invalided out of the army, so he offered the knowledge and practical experience he had gained in the army to the company. In 1922 they formed a new company, Scammell Lorries Ltd, and they became among the biggest in commercial production. They were acquired by DAF Trucks in 1988.

Scammell purchased a three-wheeled mechanical-horse design in 1933 from Napier & Son (who had previously offered it to Karrier, who turned it down). The result was a successful series of three wheelers in various forms, which were extremely popular with railway companies among others. Noted at the Streetlife Museum in Hull on 6 October 2018 was this 3-ton 1933 example built for the London & North Eastern Railway.

One of the few vehicles that were not built specifically for a railway company was this 3-ton version that was purchased from new in 1946 by Bass Breweries Ltd and was seen at the Burton-on-Trent Museum of Brewing on 3 August 2007. Note how much wider it is compared to the previous image and also the addition of the bar to the front, which acted as a stabiliser (vehicles tended to be prone to tipping when turning fully laden). This would become a standard fitting on all further models.

Built in 1934 for the Great Western Railway, this 6-ton version was seen on display at the National Railway Museum on 7 April 2012.

In the late 1940s Scammell replaced the previous vehicles with a revamped version and more defined cab front. These newer vehicles were given the name Scarab, which would remain in production for nearly twenty years until 1967, when they were redesigned again as The Townsman (which are outside the scope of this book). The company had produced approximately 30,000 three-wheeled mechanical horses when production ceased in 1968, and there are roughly 120 that survive in the hands of preservationists. This 1952-built Scarab is one of those. It was used by the Royal Air Force and sees out its days on display at the East Anglian Railway Museum at Carlton Colville, as noted on 12 August 2007.

The last vehicle that I covered in chapter one was a 1932 Stevens Brothers three-wheeled van restoration project. Noted on the same day, 29 July 2012, was this completely restored 1936 water cooled light commercial van that was built by the company.

The Raleigh Bicycle Company decided in 1934 to discontinue manufacturing their three-wheeled vehicles, so their works manager Tom Williams and fellow employee Edward Thompson built a prototype of their own in Tom's back garden. This prototype was similar to the lightweight vans built by Stevens Brothers, but had handlebars fitted (this was later changed to a steering wheel after unsuccessful trials). In 1935 Williams & Thompson left Raleigh and formed their own company: the Reliant Motor Company.

The Reliant company had been producing lightweight three-wheeler vans for forty-six years before David Jason rolled up on our television screens as Derek Trotter in his yellow Regal Supervan III. Pictured at the Lister Tyndale Steam Rally at Berkeley Castle, Gloucestershire, on 18 June 2010 was this 1948-built Regent delivery van.

These vans were known as 'girder-forked' due to their motocycle front wheel configuration. However, not all of them built by the company came in van form, as can be seen in this 25 July 2010 picture, taken at the Cannon Hall Motor Show in Barnsley, which depicts a 1950-built example as a step-sided pick-up vehicle.

4. Eight Wheelers

The heavy end of road haulage in the UK was dominated for over thirty years by the rigid eight-wheeled lorry. While this type of vehicle was manufactured in many countries in the world, it was invariably the British manufacturers that led the field in the production of these stalwarts of road haulage. Some of the main attractions for companies to purchase these lorries was they were sturdily built, efficient, safe and very balanced, thereby eliminating the possibility of any load 'shifting' during transit. They were also available in a variety of different types.

This flatbed vehicle is a DG type that was built by Foden in 1946 and was on display at the Abbey Steam Rally at Yeovil in Somerset on 29 April 2017.

Seen on 5 September 2010 at the Great Dorset Steam Fair is this 1952-built Foden FG615 type dropside vehicle, complete with load.

This particular vehicle is a short wheelbase dual-purpose dropside and tipper lorry and is a Foden type S21 (nicknamed the 'Mickey Mouse') – originally given the nicknames of 'Spaceship' and 'Sputnik' by the commercial press, when launched in 1958. This example seen at Statfold Barn Railway on 14 September 2013 was built in 1959.

The Lancashire Steam Motor Company, founded in Leyland in 1896, specialised in producing steam-powered vehicles (their first products were lawn mowers). They began producing petrol vehicles in 1905 and two years later took over a rival steam company and changed their name to Leyland Motors. They would go on to be one of the largest manufacturers of commercial vehicles and buses in the country, before becoming defunct in 1968. Built in 1936 as an Octopus flatbed, this example was seen at Winkleigh, Devon, on 7 October 2012, during an open day at the West of England Transport Collection.

The Octopus was one of the most successful lorries built by Leyland, and noted on 12 July 2014 at the Powderham Castle Historic Vehicle Gathering at Kenton, Devon, was this 1951-built tanker version.

Founded in Southall on the outskirts of London two years before the start of the First World War, the Associated Equipment Company specialised in manufacturing commercial vehicles and buses, trading under the name AEC. They lasted until 1979, when following the buyout by British Leyland they were closed.

This example of a tanker is a Mammoth Major that was built in 1951 and was noted at the Gilcombe Festival of Transport, held opposite the Haynes International Motor Museum at Sparkford, Somerset, on 10 August 2013.

Built in 1953, this Mammoth Major Mk III flatbed differs from the previous example by way of having had the front end completed remodelled. It was seen on 3 September 2010 at the Great Dorset Steam Fair in Tarrant Hinton.

By 1955 AEC had reverted back to the original design in regards to the front end of their vehicles, only differing due to the bodywork being more flush with the sides of the radiator, as this Mammoth Major flatbed, seen at Winkleigh on 7 October 2012, shows.

Yet another remodelled front end of the Mammoth Major came in 1957, as can be seen in this short wheelbase flatbed example taken at Tarrant Hinton during the Great Dorset Steam Fair on 3 September 2010.

In 1932 Edwin Richard Foden resigned from the board of directors at his father's company, Foden Trucks, aged sixty-two. He believed the future of commercial vehicles was in diesel power – Fodens were still focusing heavily on steam vehicles at the time. So, with his son and two colleagues he founded ERF Trucks in Middlewich, Cheshire (his initials forming the company name). In some countries – Australia for example – they were marketed under the name Western Star, ironically the same name as Canadian company who took them over in 1996.

This type C16 example was built by the company in 1946 and was noted at the Onslow Park Steam Rally, Shrewsbury, on 29 August 2011.

5. Articulated Tractor Units

Following the changes in legislation to the Road Transport Bill of 1963, operators of road haulage companies were given the advantage and upper hand regarding the use of articulated vehicles over the rigid eight wheelers, which would lead to the demise of those vehicles. Although there were small numbers of articulated lorries manufactured before those changes, afterwards their rise was prolific. The time of articulated lorries had finally come to the fore and would change the road haulage market throughout the UK and the rest of the world forever.

In 1866 the German company Magrius Kommanditist began manufacturing manual fire-fighting vehicles. By 1917 they began producing motorised examples of those vehicles. During the Second World War the company was taken over by Klockner Humboldt Deutz AG and became Magrius Deutz. Seen at the Tarrant Hinton Great Dorset Steam Fair on 3 September 2010 was this 1959-built Jupiter tractor unit. Note the company logo on the grill – a stylised letter 'M' with a long sharp centre point – which represents the spire of Ulm Minster, a Lutheran church in the city of Ulm (headquarters of the company).

Mack Trucks Incorporated was the new name given to the American truck manufacturing company in 1922. It was founded in June 1900 by brothers John & Augustus Mack as Mack Brothers Company.

Pictured on 12 September 2015 at the Statfold Barn Railway enthusiasts' day were these two examples. The one nearest the camera is a 1953-built LJSWX tractor unit, the one behind was built in 1991.

This 1958 B61 Thermodyne unit was seen at the Great Dorset Steam Fair on 5 September 2010. Note the bulldog logo on the side of the bonnet and sat on top of the radiator. This became the company logo in 1921 after they earned the nickname during First World War when British troops related them to the British bulldog after driving them – in that they were tenacious, durable and tough.

Built in 1950, this very impressive looking Leyland Super Hippo was being put through its paces in the ring area at the Somerset Steam Spectacular show at Low Ham, near Langport, on Saturday 17 July 2010.

Introduced by Leyland in 1958, the Super Beaver was a short wheelbase version of the Super Hippo. This 1959 example, seen on 29 August 2011 at the Onslow Park Steam Rally, would make light work of hauling the load behind it.

The Bristol Tramways & Carriage Company was founded in 1908. Although buses were their mainstay, they also manufactured commercial vehicles and in 1943 that branch of the company was separated out into Bristol Commercial Vehicles Ltd. They were finally closed when taken over by Leyland in 1983. This former British Road Services-owned vehicle is a type HA6L that was built in 1956 and was noted on 7 August 2010 at the Gloucestershire Steam Extravaganza, which was was held on the Kemble airfield site.

Wolverhampton-based company Guy Motors Ltd was founded in 1914, building cars, commercial vehicles, buses and trolleybuses. In 1961 Jaguar Cars bought the company and they experienced the same problems that later befell the parent company (in regards to the numerous mergers, etc), and eventually became defunct in 1982. Pictured at a pre-auction viewing in Taunton on 17 February 1990 is this very sorry looking 1953-built Otter tractor unit.

On display at the Great Dorset Steam Fair on 3 September 2010 was this 1926 S10 six-wheeled arctic. This was the first type of commercial vehicle that was built by Scammell Lorries. It was designed and developed by Lt Col Alfred Scammell, who had been made managing director when the company moved to Watford from Spitalfields in London in 1920.

This vehicle is a type 'QC' and was a collaboration between Bedford and Scammell that was first introduced for the War Office in 1939. It comprises of a short wheelbase Bedford vehicle, with Scammell quick coupling turntable gear. Scammell also supplied the semi-trailers (seen here) for these vehicles. This particular example was built in 1952 and was pictured at the World of Country Life Museum, during their Fantastic Historic Vehicles Event on 14 September 2014.

Introduced in 1954 and available for the next twelve years afterwards, the ERF 'KV' type was easily recognisable by its an oval-shaped grille and curved wrap around split two-part windscreen. On 5 September 2010 at the Great Dorset Steam Fair in Tarrant Hinton, this 1956-built example was one of the numerous vehicles on display.

Maurice Rowe was a coach builder and owner of Rowe's Garage in Dobwalls, Cornwall. In 1953 he formed M. G. Rowe (Motors) Doublebois Ltd and designed and built several types of lorries that would be ideally suited to handle the many Cornish hills; these vehicles were marketed under the brand name of Hillmaster. Everything was built by Rowe except for the cabs, which were Rowe designed and made by the coachbuilders Jennings from Sandbach, Cheshire. Due to poor sales the company was wound up in 1963. Seen at the Launceston Steam & Vintage Rally on 24 May 2015 was this 1957 example.

6. Ballast Tractors

Ballast tractors are vehicles that have been specially weighted by adding ballast over the driving wheels to maximise traction. These types of vehicles are primarily used to haul exceptionally large heavy trailer loads, examples of which include oil-rig modules, bridge sections, industrial turbines and even fairground rides on occasions. They are built using a reinforced heavy-duty chassis, which has to take the extra weight of the ballast. Most of this type of vehicles have high-powered, low-geared engines that give substantial torque at low speeds. Many are fitted with heavy-duty hub reduction axles to maximise the low speeds required to move their loads.

This is a type TS3 QX, built by Commer in 1959 as an articulated tractor unit, but it was soon converted to a 10-ton ballast tractor, and it was seen in this guise on 29 April 2017 at the Abbey Hill Steam Rally in Yeovil.

Built by Leyland Motors in 1949, this Beaver Autotractor Ballast Unit was on display at the Great Dorset Steam Fair on 5 September 2010. Note the heavy-duty towing bar on the front, which would have been used to recover stricken vehicles bogged down on soft surfaces or similar.

One of the more popular of the Atkinson-built vehicles was the Borderer, of which this 1952-built example ballast tractor is one. It was taken on 1 January 2000 at Taunton, prior to taking part in the annual New Years' Day Vintage Road Run, organised by the Somerset Traction Engine Club.

The vast majority of ballast tractors were used either by showmen for towing funfair rides/circus equipment or by heavy haulage companies to tow oversize large/awkward loads. This 1952-built Scammell MV20 was used by a South Wales haulage company, and was looking immaculate when displayed at the Gloucestershire Steam Extravaganza that took place on the airfield at Kemble on 7 August 2010.

Gleaming in the bright summer sunshine on 3 September 2010 at the Great Dorset Steam Fair, ahead of spending the afternoon hauling a 150-ton steam locomotive around the site, this 1957 Scammell Junior constructor was new to Pickfords. It is preserved in its original condition.

Seen at the Somerset Steam Spectacular at Low Ham on 17 July 2010 is this 1942-built Bedford OXC type ballast tractor. Interestingly it was in a black and red livery when pictured and carried branding M&G King and Daughter, Taunton, Somerset. Four years later it had been painted into maroon and red and rebranded to M. Osborne & Sons Contractors, Woodbury. In August 2018, noted at another show, it had been rebranded again to A&D Recovery Spares & Repairs, Northwood. It is unknown to the author whether the different brandings are because the vehicle has been sold on to new owners or not.

This 1957 ERF-built type KV ballast tractor is used by a showman to tow the living van (seen on the right) and a funfair carousel ride. It was seen soaking up the 3 September 2010 afternoon summer sunshine at the Great Dorset Steam Fair.

7. Cattle Trucks, Horse Boxes/Livestock Carriers

Cattle, horses, geese, pigs, sheep, chickens and other livestock found on farms have been conveyed from one location to another in vehicles along the roads of Britain for hundreds of years. In the days that preceded motorised vehicles, a farmer would often take his produce or livestock to market in a farm cart pulled by a horse or ox, and it would not have been uncommon for the farmer to sell the horse or ox (and occasionally the cart) and then walk home. The vehicles used to transport animals in the twenty-first century are specifically built high-tech ones.

Noted on 1 March 2014 at the Basingstoke Milestones Museum is this 1930 locally built Thornycroft Ltd type A2 cattle wagon. Note the small slatted square at the rear of the cab. This was so the herdsman, travelling with the driver, could check on the welfare of the animals while being transported.

Commercial Vehicles Built Before 1960

33

Another Thornycroft cattle truck was this much later and more modern 1959-built Swift example, which was noted at the Abbey Hill Steam Rally, held on the outskirts of Yeovil, on 6 May 2013.

This immaculately and beautifully restored TS3 cattle truck, noted in the Dorset sunshine on 7 July 2013 at the Chickerell Steam & Vintage Show held at the hamlet of Knights-in-the-Bottom, was built by Commer in 1959.

The Gloucestershire Steam Extravaganza on 7 August 2010 was the location for this preserved 1954 Leyland Motors-built Comet 90 luxury horse box.

In 1908 William Durant had a dream, that one company could have several 'marques' under its ownership with each one being independent of the others. Along with Robert McLaughlin, he founded the General Motors Holding Company, in which thirteen car companies and ten parts and accessories manufacturers were consolidated into one. These mass acquisitions left the company with a cash shortfall and in 1910 Durant was forced out of the company.

Undeterred by this, in 1911 he teamed up with Swiss race car driver/engineer Louis Chevrolet and formed the Chevrolet Motor Car Company. Using Chevrolet to acquire a controlling stake in GMC and by means of a reverse merger in 1918, Durant once again took the helm of the company he had co-founded in 1908. However, his tenure would only last until 1920 when he was ousted again.

Following the First World War the company decided that the Chevrolet brand was to compete with Henry Ford's Model TT, and began producing commercial vehicles at that time. One of the popular types of commercial vehicles built under the Chevrolet banner was the type AK. This 1946-built example was manufactured as a small livestock conveying vehicle, and was noted on 1 January 2016 at the annual Somerset Traction Engine Clubs' New Year's Day Vintage Road Run.

Participating in the Historical Commercial Vehicle Societies' annual London to Brighton Run on 1 May 2016, this WLG type livestock carrier was built by Bedford in 1936. It was pictured on Brighton Road, Purley in Surrey.

Another WLG is this 1937-built horse box, on display at the Great Dorset Steam Fair on 5 September 2010.

Easily one of the most recognisable of Bedford's vehicles was the 'O' type. Noted on the same day and location as the previous picture was this 1947-built example of a horse box.

This beautifully restored 'O' type cattle truck was seen at the Somerset Steam Spectacular near Langport on 17 July 2010. It was built by the Luton-based company in 1952.

Another vehicle seen at the Great Dorset Steam Fair on 5 September 2010 was this 1952-built Bedford, this one being an OLA2 type horse box.

8. Drays and Flatbeds

These vehicles are among the most versatile of commercial vehicles used on Britain's roads. They are used to carry any number of different commodities ranging from planks of wood to the 'lift on/off' bulk freight containers used by the railway companies. Numerous examples were acquired by breweries and milk companies, which were then fitted with upright vertical poles and removeable chains and used as drays for making deliveries to public houses, working men's/social clubs and dairies.

Thomas Murray and Norman Fulton founded the Albion Motor Car Company in Biggar, South Lanarkshire, in 1899. After ten years of car production the company decided to concentrate their business on the commercial vehicle side of the market, and as a result of that decision the company name was changed to Albion Motors Ltd. In 1951 the company was purchased by Leyland Motors, who continued to use the Albion brand until 1972.

The first commercial vehicle built by the company was the A14, which was a 32-hp 3-ton rear wheel chain-driven model, large numbers of which were supplied to the War Office during the First World War. This example was built in 1914 and was noted at the National Motor Museum in Beaulieu on 6 December 2014, sporting Ringwood Brewery decals, having been converted to a brewers dray.

Horace & John Dodge were inseparable brothers throughout their childhood and adult lives. In 1901 they went into business as the Dodge Brothers Company, as a machine shop producing various automobile parts. Within their first year of trading they had secured a lucrative contract to manufacture transmissions for the Olds Motor Vehicle Company. The company enjoyed continued success and in 1914 they produced their own car under the Dodge brand and renamed the company The Dodge Brothers Motor Company. Following the death of both brothers in 1920, John in January (influenza) and Horace in December (cirrhosis of the liver/pneumonia), their widows sold the company to an investment group in 1925, who sold it to the Chrysler Corporation in 1928. Chrysler continued to market vehicles under the Dodge name and the brand is still produced in 2021.

The company began producing commercial vehicles in 1929, and by 1933 they had opened a factory in Kew, London, under Dodge Motors UK. This type 300 COE (cab over engine) flatbed was built there in 1958. It was seen on 29 August 2011 at the Onslow Park Steam Rally in Shrewsbury.

In Coventry in 1902 Cyril Maudslay went into business making marine internal combustion engines under the name of Maudslay Motors. The engines sales were poor but in 1903 the development of a three-cylinder camshaft engine so impressed the City of London Corporation that they commissioned a 12-ton petrol railway locomotive to transport meat trucks to Deptford meat market (which included a 1 in 36 gradient). The locomotive was an ultimate success and car and commercial production was soon to follow. With the outbreak of war private car production was stopped and the company supplied a number of 3-, 5- and 6-ton lorries to the War Office.

This example of a flatbed, seen on 5 September 2010 at the Great Dorset Steam Fair, was built in 1950 as a Mogul III type. Note how the front end is similar to those on the AEC Matador series – due to the AEC buy out of Maudslay two years previously.

At the tail end of 1901 Henry Ford founded the Henry Ford Company. By August 1902 Henry sold the company to the Cadillac Motor Company – although keeping the rights to his name. The following year at the age of thirty-nine, with backing from twelve investors (two major ones being John and Horace Dodge), he launched the Ford Motor Company with $28,000. Early investors were concerned that the company might not prove to be a success; however, those fears were unfounded and Henry turned a company that was producing a meagre few cars a day into what would become a worldwide multi-million-pound one that is still producing cars.

1909 saw the company branching out into the commercial vehicles market, the first model being a lightweight truck version of their successful car (the Model 'T' of which 15 million were produced between 1909 and 1927), which was named the Model TT. This flatbed example, seen at the Great Dorset Steam Fair on 3 September 2010, was built in 1923.

During the First World War, in order to help with the war effort, Ford started to manufacture a range of general purpose tractors, and in order to separate them from the automobile business they were built under the name Fordson. The United Kingdom arm of the company (Ford of Britain) also manufactured commercial vehicles under the Fordson name until 1964. This flatbed is a type 7V that was built at Dagenham, Essex, in 1944 and was taking part in the Great Dorset Steam Fair on 5 September 2010.

Ford of Britain introduced another range in 1949 under the Thames marque. One of the first designs released under this new marque was the E83W, the front end of which bears a resemblance to the Anglia/Popular 'sit up and beg'-style saloons made by the company. This example was built in 1955 and was seen at the Statfold Barn Railway Enthusiasts Day at Tamworth on 19 September 2010.

The second vehicle to appear under the Thames name was the 'ET6', this particular example is a 4D, it was built in 1956 and is a dray that would have collected milk churns (like the ones shown), to/from railway stations and villages to the dairies and bottling plants. It was seen on 3 September 2010 taking part in the Great Dorset Steam Fair.

The most successful of the Thames range was undoubtedly the Trader, which was introduced in 1957. This milk dray example is a Mk II that was built in 1959 and was on display at Sparkford in Somerset on 10 August 2013 at the Gilcombe Festival of Transport.

Manchester brothers Francis and William formed Crossley Brothers in 1867, manufacturing oil and gas fired internal combustion engines. In April 1906 the automobile arm of the business was formed as a separate entity: Crossley Motors Ltd. The company went on to enjoy moderate success, manufacturing some 19,000 high-quality cars until 1938, over 5,500 buses between 1926 and 1958 and 21,000 commercial and military vehicles from 1914 to 1945. The company was acquired by AEC in the late 1940s, but bus production under the Crossley marque lasted until 1958.

One of the last designs built before the takeover was the 3-ton front-wheel-drive '4x4' General Service Vehicle. This flatbed example awaits restoration at the West of England Transport Collection in Winkleigh, Devon, and was noted on 6 October 2013 during the annual held open day.

During 1905 while running Wolseley Tool & Motor Car Company Ltd, jointly founded in 1901 with Thomas and Albert Vickers, Herbert Austin had a major falling out with the two brothers over engine design. Gaining financial backing from steel magnate Frank Kayser, Austin was able to get the Austin Motor Company up and running. The company were direct competition to Morris Motors Ltd and there was a healthy rivalry between the two companies.

The company produced its first commercial vehicle in 1913, a 2-ton lorry, but it wasn't until the hostilities began in 1939 that the commercial aspect of their manufacturing really took off. One of their more successful commercial designs was the 'K' series, production of which began at the start of the Second World War. This example is a 1948-built K4 flatbed, which was noticed at Low Ham near Langport during the Somerset Steam Spectacular on 17 July 2010.

Dudley businessman Absolom Harper founded iron foundry A. Harper & Sons in 1822. George Bean had married Harper's granddaughter in 1901 and became the principal shareholder. Six years later he became the chairman when Absolom retired due to poor health, the company becoming A. Harper & Sons & Bean. The company had been producing automobile parts in the years prior to the First World War, and managed to secure a contract to supply shell casings and shrapnel to the government for the war, making over 21,000 a week during 1916. At the cessation of hostilities the manufacturing rights for the pre-war 'Perry' car (built by the Perry Motor Company between 1913 and 1916), were up for sale so the company purchased them and became A. Harper, Sons & Bean Ltd. They began automobile manufacturing using 'Bean' as the trade marque name. In 1924 they embarked on the construction of commercial vehicles.

Built in 1926, this long wheelbase 14-hp dray was pictured on 29 July 2012, at the Black Country Living Museum in Dudley.

After the First World War in 1919 Foster & Seddon Ltd formed in Pendleton, Lancashire, as a servicing and distribution of commercial vehicles business. After eighteen years the company decided that they would manufacture their own commercial vehicles and ten years later they changed their name to Seddon Lorries, moving to Oldham. They would continue making commercial vehicles until 1970 when they bought out Atkinson Vehicles Ltd and became Seddon-Atkinson Vehicles Ltd. Four years later they were acquired by International Harvester.

Noted at the Gloucestershire Steam Extravaganza on 7 August 2010, this Mk V flatbed was built by the company in 1955.

9. Dropsided Vehicles

These vehicles come in various sizes, ranging from small pick-up types up to 7.5-ton and above full-size lorries. They are a versatile means of transporting goods (although not as versatile as the vehicles in the previous chapter), but nevertheless they are an extremely useful vehicle for companies to own and use in their business.

Edward Lisle of Wolverhampton began making bicycles in the early 1870s and in 1896 he had formed the Star Cycle Company. The following year the company had purchased a Benz 3.5-hp motor car and Lisle decided that maybe this was the way forward. So using the Benz as a basis for a design of their own cars, the Star Motor Company was formed in 1898 as a separate entity to the bicycle production. During the First World War, the company came under the ownership of the British government and they began manufacturing commercial vehicles for the British, French and Russian armies, although the companies' main output during this time was to produce aircraft wings and parts for mines.

Pictured at the Onslow Park Steam Rally in Shrewsbury on 29 August 2011, this 1929-built Star Flyer drop-sided version has been repainted into the livery seen here. It was previously in dark blue with yellow writing, and it was used in an episode of the BBC hit comedy show *Dad's Army*.

At the turn of the twentieth century in Cleveland, Ohio, the Peerless Motor Car Company was formed, where they began producing De Dion Bouton cars (under license from the French company), before embarking in 1902 on the manufacturing of their own designed vehicles. Like numerous other companies they began producing commercial vehicles for the military during the First Word War. The majority of these consisted of the 'armoured vehicle', a chassis shipped to England for the British Army and fitted with armoured bodies that were made by the Austin Motor Company.

Pictured on 18 May 2013 at the Wheal Martyn China Clay Museum in Carthew, Cornwall, this is a 1916-built example of a former armoured vehicle. It was purchased after hostilities ceased by Parkyn & Peters Ltd, who were china clay producers in St Austell, who rebuilt it into the dropsided version seen here.

A thirty-minute train journey south-west from Zurich, Switzerland, will bring you to the town of Olten, the base of the 1902 formed Schweizerische Automobil Fabrik Berna, a manufacturer of small numbers of motor cars under the Berna marque. In 1905 they began concentrating on building buses, trolleybuses and commercial vehicles, and within a year they changed name to Motor-Werke Berna AG. After nearly going under in 1907, the company somehow came under English ownership in 1908, before being bought back by Swiss shareholders in 1912, becoming Motorwagenfabrik Berna AG. Following the depression in the 1920s the company hit financial difficulties and in 1929 the Swiss firm of Adolph Saurer AG acquired a majority stake in the company (which they owned outright in 1976).

This example is a L4 dropsided version that was built by the company in 1958 and was seen taking part in the annual Historic Commercial Vehicle Societies' London to Brighton Run at Purley, Surrey, on 1 May 2016.

In 1919 the Manchester firm Crossley Motors Ltd and the American company Willys-Overland Motors formed a jointly owned company – namely Willys Overland Crossley Ltd – who would have factories in Stockport, Berlin and Antwerp, where cars, buses and commercial vehicles would be manufactured. The basis for their vehicle production was that the chassis and running gear would be shipped from Willy's Canadian plant and Crossley's would build all the bodywork and fit the engines. The relationship between Crossley's and Willys started to sour in 1931 and the jointly owned company went into voluntary liquidation in 1933.

They built their first commercial vehicle in 1924, which was a 1-ton model. Two years later this was upgraded to a 30-cwt model, which were launched under the Manchester brand name, and would do so until closure. This 1929 example is a 30/35 cwt Model B1, which was pictured at the Joe Nemeth Engineering Public Open Day in Easter Compton on 2 October 2010.

In Chicago in 1905 C. A. Tilt founded the Diamond 'T' Motor Car Company, his shoemaker father designed a logo for his shop, which was a large capital letter 'T' (for the family name), within a diamond shape, signifying quality. The company began by producing luxury touring cars up to 70 hp and between its inception and 1911 six different models had been produced, but sales of these were fairly poor, so in 1912 the company focused all its efforts on producing commercial vehicles, which was a huge turning point for them and they were to go on to manufacture huge numbers of military vehicles especially.

The company only built two other models apart from military vehicles. These were the Model 80 and Model 201. This example is one of the former and was built in 1937 as a dropsided pick-up version. It is seen on display on a sunny, but heavily overcast, 2 October 2010 at Joe Nemeth Engineering in Easter Compton.

At the end of the First World War in 1919, French industrialist André-Gustave Citroën founded the Citroën Automobile Company in Paris, and began to manufacture cars under the Citroën name – a marque which, despite several changes in ownership, is still produced in large quantities over a hundred years later. In October 1926 the company launched its first commercial vehicle, the 1,000 kg B15 model, which like all subsequent models was widely appreciated due to its reliability and robust strength.

Seen on 29 May 2016 at the La Vie En Bleu event held at The Prescott Hillclimb in Gotherington, Gloucestershire, this 1951-built dropside U23 model had the same front end as the companies' big selling Traction Avant saloon cars.

On 7 October 2012, hidden among some trolleybuses at the West of England Transport Collection Open Day, was this Fourgon type 55 dropsided vehicle built by Citroën in c. 1954.

During the late 1920s, brothers Alan and Richard Jensen, from West Bromwich, West Midlands, went to work for lorry body manufacturers Walter J. Smith & Sons. In 1934 Walter passed away and the two brothers managed to acquire a controlling shareholding in the company and changed the name to Jensen Motors Ltd, a name that would be around for another forty-two years, becoming synonymous and famous for producing luxury sports cars. In the late 1930s the company branched out into commercial vehicle production and marketed them under the JNSN marque, therefore keeping the two brands separate.

The first vehicles produced under this name were lightweight aluminium trucks, which were very well received. Production was halted during the Second World War, and the company concentrated on producing turrets for tanks and a range of specialised ambulances and fire engines. Production of commercial vehicles resumed at the end of the hostilities. This example was built in 1951 as a Freighter 6-ton vehicle. It was seen at the Onslow Park Steam Rally on 29 August 2011.

Seen at the Launceston Steam & Vintage Rally on 24 May 2015, this 8-ton long wheelbase dropsided lorry was built in 1958 by the short-lived company of Rowe as one of their Hillmaster vehicles. As you can see by comparing it to the version covered in chapter five, externally the only difference is the modified grille.

10. Ice Cream and Hot Food Vans

The difference between these types of vehicle is that the majority of ice cream vans are factory purpose built, whereas many hot food vans are conversions from standard panel vans. Since the basic layouts of both types are almost identical, this makes them a viable, fairly inexpensive vehicle to convert if you wish to go into business using them.

Between 1906 and 1955 Jowett Cars Ltd built light cars and commercial vehicles in Bradford, West Yorkshire, the company had been in business since 1901, when brothers Benjamin and William Jowett made the switch from bicycle to motor vehicle production. Built in 1949, this Bradford ice cream van was pictured just after a downpour on the Royal Albert Dock in Liverpool on 16 July 2016. The name came from the town where the vehicles were produced.

Pictured on 4 October 2015 at the West of England Transport Collection, Winkleigh, Devon, this 1955-built Karrier Bantam mobile cafeteria conversion is in much need of restoration to bring it back to its former glory.

In 1947 Citroën introduced the H-Type (often called HY), general purpose panel van and built them until 1981. However, the past ten years or so has seen their revival and popularity boom, this resurgence coming from many being converted into fast-food mobile catering vehicles.

This 1956-built example is owned by the West Country based Little Van Rouge company and it is used as a bespoke catering and coffee bar. It was rescued from a farmyard among rusting farm machinery in the south of France in 2013 and has been lovingly and painstakingly restored, as noticed in this 1 July 2017 picture taken at the Blackmore Vale Revival Show at Henstridge, Somerset.

Another 1956 H-type also being used as a coffee and cake bar is this example that was noted on 18 August 2018 not far from the London Eye and Westminster Bridge.

The Morris PV was introduced by the company in 1939 as a forward control vehicle for primary use by the army. This 1953 example was formerly a military ambulance, which was converted into this ice cream van during the 1990s. It was noted on 5 May 2014 during the Historic Festival of Transport held at Donington racecourse.

Noted at Gotherington adjacent to the Gloucestershire Warwickshire Steam Railway ahead of the day's working on 7 August 2010, this is a 1958-built Morris 'J' type ice cream van.

Taken almost nine years after the previous image on 16 July 2019 at St James's Park in London, following a complete body rebuild and repaint, this is the same 1958-built vehicle as the previous picture.

Built in 1959 as a Morris 1-ton truck, this vehicle, noted at Chatham Historic Dockyard during a Medway Festival of Steam & Transport show on 24 April 2014, was converted for use as an ice cream van during the mid-1970s.

Clifford Partridge & Ross Wilson got together in 1926 as Partridge Wilson Engineering in Leicester, producing Davenset radios. Four years later with a workforce of seven, they began manufacturing battery chargers. In 1934 they began production of battery-electric road vehicles, which were marketed under the Wilson Electric marque. This move saw the company expand rapidly to the point that just after the Second World War, they had some 500 employees. They made these road vehicles until 1954, but continued to produce chargers and rectifiers for another twenty years after that.

Built in 1935 for the Coventry Corporation's Electricity Department as a milk float, this vehicle was converted to an ice cream van in 1947. It was seen on 23 June 2012 at the Snibston Discovery Park Museum in Leicester.

The pug-nosed Bedford 'CA' was a light commercial utility van that was introduced by the company in 1952 and was manufactured until 1969. This example was built in 1958 and converted during the 1970s to the guise seen here at Toddington station on the Gloucestershire Warwickshire Steam Railway on a sunny 18 August 2011.

This rather odd-looking Luton van, seen at East Huntspill during the 2016 Blue Ridge Runners All Makes Motor Show, was built by Ford in 1951 as a F-1 0.5-ton pick-up truck, which was converted by its owner to be used as a rear-serving coffee wagon.

11. Luton Lorries and Vans

These vehicles are basically a box type of vehicle. They are comprised of a chassis (lorry or van) that is fitted with a box that extends over the top of the cab – this part is often referred to as 'the kick'. This extension gives a little extra storage capacity within the box. These vehicles are very popular with firms whose business involves moving people's furniture from one home/location to another, and more often than not 'the kick' is used to store all those small boxes/items, thereby leaving the majority of the box for the larger and bulkier items of furniture, household appliances and belongings.

Pictured on a sunny 6 May 2013 in Yeovil, Somerset, during the Abbey Hill Steam Rally, this 1949 Basingstoke-built Thornycroft Nippy Star was fitted with a Luton body, carrying Uttoxeter firm Elkes Biscuits two-tone blue livery.

For a vehicle that had lain in an overgrown garden for almost thirty years, this ex-British Road Services, 1949-built Commer Q2 Superpoise Luton lorry wasn't looking as bad as one may expect. It was noted during the pre-auction viewing of the Teddy Tucker Collection in Taunton, Somerset, on 17 February 1990.

Noted at the West of England Transport Collection at Winkleigh on 6 October, this 1932-built Leyland Llama Luton lorry is in need of some TLC and light restoration work.

Bearing John Lewis Partnership livery on 29 July 2012 during Black Country Manufacturers Festival at the Dudley Black Country Museum is this 1949 Guy Wolf Luton van. Note the Native American head logo sited on top of the radiator.

As previously mentioned in this book, the Bedford 'O' type is one of the most easily recognisable. The Luton body gets its name from the town where this company was based. The style of the design was to accommodate the high-volume low weight loads of straw hats, which were a major part of Luton's commerce and industry. The hats were wrapped in long cylinders and hessian fabric, which fitted across the width of the van. All of the earliest Luton bodies were fitted onto Bedford vehicles, with other companies following.

The free Regent Street Motor Show in London is held on the last Saturday in October. One of the regular firms that put on a display every year is Abel's Furniture & Removals Company, of which this 1941 'O' type is always a regular feature, seen here on 31 October 2015.

'Something Good from Bury' is the slogan on the front of this vehicle, which relates to the Benson's Quality Sweets (not the vehicle as that came from Sandbach). It was built in 1959 by ERF as a KV 44GK type, seen on 7 August 2010 at Kemble Airfield during the Gloucestershire Steam Extravaganza.

Early in April 1952 two of Britain's biggest motor companies (Morris & Austin), after spending years in direct competition with each other, joined together in a venture to rescue the flailing English car market, and the British Motor Corporation Ltd was founded, with both companies' vehicles still being produced and carrying their own names individually.

One of the newer designs to come from the merger came in the form of the Morris LD van, of which this 1958-built Luton example is one, which was seen during the Great Dorset Steam Fair on 5 September 2010.

12. Rigid Box Vehicles

These lorries are usually rated as having a tare weight between 7.5 and 12 ton and they are vehicles that have a box body mounted onto a chassis, but do not have the extension covered in the vehicles in the previous chapter. In more recent years, however, this type of lorry has been replaced by the more popular curtain sided vehicles – due to these being easier to load and unload – so therefore numbers of these vehicles being used have declined.

The Foden FG type was released in 1948, this example (built in 1955), pictured on 22 August 2009 at the Waltham Abbey Royal Gunpowder Mills Museum, was used by the Army as an ammunition carrier. Note the 18-inch thick solid reinforced separate steel section, behind the cab, which was designed in case any of the ammunition carried in the box body should explode and therefore reduce the risk of serious injuries to the driver and passenger.

Sunny Sparkford in Somerset during the Gilcombe Festival of Transport on 10 August 2013 saw this 1959-built Foden S21 six-wheeler rigid box vehicle looking resplendent as the sun beams down on it.

This Dennis Pax type II was pictured on 17 July 2010 at the Somerset Steam Spectacular held near Langport. It was built by the company in 1958 as a 3-ton vehicle.

This 1919 Leyland RAF type box van was taking part in the Annual HCVS London to Brighton Run on 1 May 2016 on Brighton Road in Purley. Note the original solid rubber tyres.

Onslow Park Steam Rally in Shrewsbury on 29 August 2011 had a special display comprising of several Leyland trucks. This 1934 Badger was one of those. The reason for the tarpaulin over the back of the vehicle is a rather unusual one, as the top half of the box section could be removed and the vehicle used as an open type. with a drop-down flap at the rear (the sides, however, remained rigid).

Built in 1938 by Commer, this N1 type van was used by the London & North Eastern Railway as a parcels truck. It can be seen on display at the National Railway Museum in York, where it was pictured on 17 July 2012.

13. Showmans Vehicles

The years following the First World War in 1918 right through to the years leading up to and the decade or so following the Second World War were a thriving time for the travelling circuses and funfairs in Britain. They would turn up in vast numbers on the local village green or town recreation park where they would 'set up shop', so to speak, for a week or two. One of the most important aspect of these travelling sideshows would invariably be the vehicles that were used to carry all the equipment/rides/stalls, etc., required to make the attraction popular. These vehicles are known as 'Showmans' and they are also used for towing the trailers of equipment, generators for the rides and living accommodation for the performers and staff. The original vehicles were mostly steam-powered traction engines. These were replaced over time by diesel lorries – many of which had been built purposefully to carry a specific ride/attraction. Nowadays the vehicles are high tech and are more often only used to transport one particular ride/attraction, purpose-built for the job.

Carter's Steam Fair is a family run travelling vintage fairground, based in Maidenhead, Berkshire. One of their vehicles is this 1959-built Atkinson Mk 1 Black Knight eight-wheeler, which is used to carry and transport their helter-shelter and octopus rides. It is seen here on the seafront lawns in Weston-super-Mare, North Somerset, on 18 August 2012.

The Great Dorset Steam Fair on 4 September 2010 was the location of this Harris' Amusements 1959-built AEC Matador Generator vehicle.

Taken the day before the previous picture, also at the Great Dorset Steam Fair, was this Hanleys Amusements, 1960-built AEC Mercury Mk II GM4 example.

Between December 1945 and September 1948, Scammell Lorries built a total of eighteen short wheelbase 4x2 ballast tractors, given the name Showtrac. These vehicles were designed specifically for fairground use – all of these vehicles with the exception of three were given names when built. Seventeen out of the eighteen still survive and many are used frequently for the purpose that they were built for.

The first vehicle came out of the Watford factory in December 1945, and was registered as DWN 766 and named *HIS MAJESTY*. It was originally owned by Harry Studt & Sons of Swansea. On a sunny summer day (6 August 2016), I pictured it on display at the Gloucestershire Vintage & Country Extravaganza Show, held at South Cerney airfield. Note how the present owner has repainted it with the decals of the original owners.

DCO 212 *GLADIATOR* was built in 1946 for the Anderton & Rowlands travelling funfair. Seventy-four years on and the same company still owns it. It is pictured on loan at the Dingles Heritage Fairground Centre in Lifton, Devon, on 30 June 2018.

EWN 437 *GEORGE V* was another vehicle built for Studt's of Swansea, this one in 1947, who owned it until 1974, when it was purchased by a Dr Williams. This picture shows it in a far from pristine condition as it awaits sale by auction in *c.* 1991 (exact date not recorded by the author). It was taken at Cleobury Mortimer in Shropshire during the dispersal sale of Dr Williams' property. Note the living van on the left of the picture. which was also sold the same day.

The annual Great Dorset Steam Fair has a wide and varied plethora of vehicles on display and 3 September 2010 was no exception to that. Seen there that day was this 1952 ERF Type 44 Generator Wagon.

On a sunny 15 August 2010 at the Quainton Road Railway Society in Buckinghamshire, I pictured this 1959-built ERF KV type Showmans towing vehicle and living van.

14. Sidestep Pick-Ups

These vehicles differ from the dropside pick-up vehicles covered in chapter eight by the single fact that the sides on these vehicles are rigid. Among the most numerous of this type of vehicle are the American 'half-ton' style, which are very popular with 'hot rodders'.

Founded 1852 at South Bend, Indiana, as The Studebaker Brothers Manufacturing Company, makers of wagons, buggies, carriages and harnesses, by 1902 they began to manufacture automobiles under the name Studebaker Automobile Company. The marque name of Studebaker began officially in 1911 when the company refinanced and became The Studebaker Corporation. The company began production of commercial vehicles in 1929 and they remained in business until 1966.

The Blue Ridge Runners' All Makes Motor Show, held at East Huntspill in Somerset on 21 August 2016, was the location of this photograph. It shows a 1959 Transtar Model 3-E V8 0.5-ton pick-up.

Under a storm-threatening sky at the Great Dorset Steam Fair on 5 September 2010 sits this 1948-built Dodge B-1 type pick-up, whose bodywork needs a little TLC.

Chicago in 1902 saw the joining of five harvesting and agricultural companies to form the International Harvester Company. The company would manufacture a varied assortment of items, ranging from agricultural equipment to house appliances, tractors, automobiles and trucks.

Noted on a sunny 3 September 2010 at the Great Dorset Steam Fair was this 'Wagonette' pick-up vehicle, which was built by the company in 1913.

William Hillman joined Coventry Sewing Machine Company in 1858 as a skilled engineer. In 1876 Hillman left the company and following a succession of different partnerships in bicycle manufacturing, he became a millionaire before the turn of the twentieth century. In 1907 Hillman decided that he wanted to move into automobile production so he teamed up with designer Breton Louis Coatalen and Hillman-Coatalen was founded. Three years later the company changed its name to Hillman Motor Car Company.

Prior to the outbreak of the Second World War the Ministry of Supply co-ordinated with four of the major British auto-manufacturers to provide military versions of their most popular mid-sized family saloons, which involved putting a utility or pick-up body onto the chassis. The result was the Light Utility 4x2. Hillman's contribution was a 10-hp vehicle attached to the chassis of the Hillman Minx. This 1938 version was pictured on a sunny May Day bank holiday (6 May) at the 2013 Abbey Hill Steam Rally in Yeovil.

Although Ford wasn't one of the companies involved in the utility vehicle program (being an American firm), but not to miss out on the opportunity to enter the utility vehicle market, they converted a couple of their saloons into pick-up vehicles. This 1947-built VTE is a conversion of the Prefect E03A saloon and was noted at the Chickerell Stream & Vintage Show at Knights-in-the-Bottom in Dorset on 7 July 2013.

Between 1949 and 1953 the Australian wing of the Ford Motor Company produced the Anglia A494A, which was available in more various body styles than the English version (which was saloon only). The two-door coupe utility or Edwardian, the name it was marketed under, was one of those. This 1953 example was noted on display on 2 August 2014 at Norton Fitzwarren in Somerset during the West Somerset Railway Association Steam Fayre & Vintage Vehicles Rally.

The Chevrolet Advance Design (AD) series 0.5-ton sidestep pick-up was introduced in 1947, and was to be one of the most popular selling of the Chevrolet range of vehicles. This example is a 1950 AD 3100 Thriftmaster, which was on display at the Killerton House Classic Car Show in Broadclyst, Devon, during the Whitsun bank holiday weekend on 26 May 2014.

The successor to the vehicle in the previous image was the Task Force series, which Chevrolet introduced in 1955. This 1959-built Apache 32 example, pictured at the Somerset Steam Spectacular on 17 July 2010, was in need of a visit to the paint shop.

In 1909 in Pontiac, Michigan, William Durant purchased the Rapid Motor Vehicle Company and made it a subsidiary of his General Motors Company, just as he had done the previous year when he acquired the Reliance Motor Car Company. In 1911 the General Motors Truck Company was founded in order to separate the cars from the commercials side of the business. The following year the Rapid and Reliance names were dropped and the vehicles were manufactured under the GMC umbrella.

During the 1920s the Chevrolet and GMC commercial vehicles began sharing the same bodywork platform – the only major differences would be the grilles and the badges (they were after all both owned by the same company). This picture shows a GMC 'E' series on display at the West of England Open Day at Winkleigh on 6 October 2013.

The GMC 100 series was a slight variation on the Chevrolet AD, by means of having a more appealing flattened style front end. This 1955 example was pictured on 21 August 2016 at the Blue Ridge Runners All Makes Motor Show at East Huntspill in Somerset.

Between 1913 and 1922 the Fargo Motor Car Company in Chicago built a brand of truck under the Fargo marque. In 1928 the Chrysler Corporation bought the company and reintroduced the marque under the Fargo Motor Corporation, which were manufactured at the companies' Canadian factory. Built in 1936 as a 0.5-ton sidestep, this example is at the Statfold Barn Railway during their enthusiasts day on 14 September 2013 as it awaits restoration.

15. Small Goods Panel Vans

The vast numbers of these vehicles that are around shows just how popular and versatile they are, and always have been, given the varying amounts of different products that can be carried within them for any number of businesses. They are also lightweight and therefore less cumbersome, making them fairly easy to park.

Built by Albion in 1934, this vehicle, which is a LCA44 40–50 cwt, was delivered to newsagent wholesalers S. Robinson & Co. Ltd, Burslem, Stoke-on-Trent, as a mobile newspaper sorting van. It was seen at the Haynes International Motor Museum in Sparkford, Somerset, on 6 September 2015.

Born in London in 1871, Reginald Walter Maudslay left college and became an apprentice civil engineer at the Crystal Palace School of Engineering under the tutelage of Sir John Wolfe-Barry (famous for London's Tower Bridge). In 1902 Reginald decided that he wanted to become an automobile manufacturer, so with financial support from Sir John, he moved to Coventry where in 1903 he established the Standard Motor Company. The company bought out Triumph Motorcycles in 1945 and was purchased by British Leyland in 1960, with the Standard name becoming phased out in 1963.

Built by the company in 1949 as a Vanguard Phase 1 panel van, this example was pictured in Purley, Surrey, on 1 May 2016 while taking part in the HCVS London to Brighton Run.

The Polygon Engineering Works was founded in 1910 to manufacture small lightweight automobiles. A prototype was launched in 1913 and just prior to the outbreak of war in 1914, the company was renamed to Trojan Ltd – their vehicles would be marketed under the Trojan marque. However, production was halted before it could start and the company made production tools and gauges for the Ministry of Supply.

Between 1920 and 1928 the company went into partnership with Leyland Motors, during which they had built 11,000 cars and 6,700 vans. In 1930 the company had secured a major lucrative contract with tea makers Brooke Bond to manufacture a substantial size fleet of delivery vans. The company continued to produce commercial vehicles until war broke out in 1939. Then they concentrated on making bomb racks and parachute containers and resumed van production in 1946.

This model, known as the 'Victory', was built by the company in 1938 and was noted on 1 May 2016 taking part in the HCVS London to Brighton Run. It was seen in Purley.

Built by Ford of Britain in 1956, under the Thames marque, was this 300E van (the front was the same design as used on the Anglia/Popular saloon cars made by the company at that time). It was noted on 7 August 2010 at the Gloucestershire Steam Extravaganza held on Kemble Airfield.

As mentioned earlier in this book, there was a resurgence of the Citroën H van as hot food conversions, but not all of them are so treated. This 1959 example has been turned into a mobile camping van and has been fitted with two single beds, a fridge, an oven and a roof rack. It was noted on 21 August 2016 at the Blue Ridge Runners All Makes Motor Show in East Huntspill, Somerset. The owner intends to keep it in its 'rat-rod'/rustic-looking condition.

Introduced in 1948 by Citroën as a front-wheel-drive economy car was the 2CV (which went on to become one of the icons in the automobile industry), they were built until 1990 and some 3.8 million were produced. The success of the car resulted in many variants (Ami, Dyane, Mehari, etc), and in total the company manufactured 9 million 2CVs and variants.

One of those variants was the AZU Fourgonnette panel van. This example was noted at the Powderham Castle Historic Vehicle Show on 12 July 2014, which was built in 1957.

During the late 1950s and through to the early 1970s, the Bedford CA Utility van was a very popular commercial vehicle and could be seen in their hundreds on Britain's roads. This example was built in 1957 and was noted on display at the Historic Vehicle Gathering in the grounds of Powderham Castle in Devon on 12 July 2014.

One of the newer and probably shortest lasting commercial vehicle manufacturers was Motor Traction Limited, who were based in New Addington, Surrey. They were founded in 1951 as Wagon Rutland Limited in Croydon. The company specialised in manufacturing commercial vehicles between 3 and 15 tons, with the chassis built to the customer's specific requirements, using the major components of other manufacturers for the rest. The shareholders liquidated the company in 1958 due mainly to sales not being as good as they had hoped they would be.

This example was built in 1952 as a 2-ton M4 type laundry van and is one of the very few surviving vehicles from the company (possibly the only one). It was seen at the Gilcombe Festival of Transport held at Sparkford on 10 August 2013.

16. Tankers and Corporation Vehicles

These vehicles are possibly among the often overlooked type, yet these forgotten 'heroes' are just as much vital a part of the commercial vehicles scene as the rest of the types covered in earlier chapters.

Built by Dennis in 1938 for the Dublin Corporation, this Ace Vacuum Tanker was used for the collection of leaves and small debris from the cities' streets. It can be found on display in the National Transport Museum at Castle Howth on the outskirts of Dublin. It was pictured there on 3 April 2015.

Built by Leyland Motors in 1938, this Lynx tanker was one of ten purchased by ESSO and numbered 5473 in their fleet. It is fairly certain that during the Second World War it was commandeered by the Ministry of Supply to carry out work required for the war effort. Due to the shortages of commercial vehicles after the war, it was used quite extensively until it became uneconomical to run and was destined for the scrapyard during the 1960s/70s. However, it was saved from that fate and restored. On Brighton Road in Purley, Surrey, on 1 May 2016 it was taking part in the annual London to Brighton Run, organised by the HCVS.

This K41 type tanker was built in 1919 by the General Motors Company, has survived the ravages of time and was in a fairly good condition for a ninety-year-old commercial vehicle when seen on 3 September 2010 at the Great Dorset Steam Fair.

This 2-ton petrol Freighter was built by Shelvoke & Drewry in 1930 as a refuse collection vehicle. It was acquired by the Cheltenham Corporation of Municipal Offices in August of that year. It was purchased from the corporation in 1948 by Wallace Margrett of Red House Farm in Elmstone Hardwicke, Gloucestershire. It had been converted to an animal feed carrier and had been barn stored for many years. It was pictured on 24 August 2012 ahead of the farm dispersal sale. Note the unusual centre single seat position in the small but compact driving cab.

This is another Shelvoke & Drewry 2-ton petrol Freighter, which was purchased by the Cheltenham Corporation in the November of its build year (1935) and registered as a refuse collection vehicle. It was purchased at the same time as the previous picture by the same gentleman, and was converted as a hay and straw carrier for use on the farm, where it was pictured on 24 August 2012. Note the unusual placing of the engine, which covers the width of the vehicle, beside and beneath where the driver sits.

Carrying Shell-Mex/BP (British Petroleum) livery while taking part in the annual HCVS London to Brighton Run, seen going along Brighton Road, Purley in Surrey on 1 May 2016, is this SA tanker, which was built by Bedford in 1954.

Built by Dennis in 1948 as an open refuse collector, this example was noted on 8 September 2013 at Westpoint, near Exeter in Devon. It was taking part in the Historic Vehicle Rally, which was organised by The West Country Historic Omnibus & Transport Trust.

17. Timber Trucks

During the 1930s through to the 1960s, sawmills were found in the vast majority of towns and cities throughout the UK, and they were a thriving commodity. These vehicles were used to drag and lift the larger heavier tree trunks in order for them to be put into position at the saw in preparation for cutting. A couple of these vehicles were covered earlier in this book in chapter four, others will be covered in this chapter.

In Marseille, France, in 1898, engineer Georges Latil and mechanic Alois Korn joined together to form the company La Société Korn et Latil. In 1903 they moved 6 km north-west of Paris to a small commune at Levallois-Perret, the company becoming Avant-Train Latil. Five years later Charles Blum joined the company and the name was changed to the rather lengthy Compagnie Française de Mécanique et d'Automobile – Avant-Train Latil.

The company specialised in four-wheel-drive vehicles for use by the military and in agriculture. This example is a Traulier Mk II, which is a winch-fitted timber truck for use in forestries. It was built in 1938 and was seen at the Great Dorset Steam Fair on 5 September 2010.

Pictured on 29 April 2017 at the Abbey Hill Steam Rally in Yeovil was another 1938 Latil truck, this example being an Industrial heavy-duty forestry winch version.

During the Second World War the Canadian Chevrolet truck division of General Motors began producing vehicles, which were specifically for use by the Canadian Armed Forces. These vehicles were classified as Canadian Military Pattern (CMP) trucks and would range from 8 cwt up to 3 tons in three different types – 4x4, 4x2 and 6x4. Following the end of the hostilities many of these vehicles were sold to private companies. This example, seen at the 2010 Great Dorset Steam Fair on 5 September, is a C60L 4x4, which has been converted for use as a timber truck. It was built in 1944.

Founded in London during 1934, Universal Power Drives specialised in the manufacturing of 4x4 forestry logging trucks, marketed under the Unipower marque. The company lasted until 1977, which included a brief period in the mid-1960s in sports car production. They were taken over by Caterpillar Incorporated.

Taken on 6 July 2014 at the Chiltern Traction Engine Club Steam Rally, held at Prestwood, Buckinghamshire, hauling some substantial size trees, this was a 1937-built Model G vehicle.

The Forester model was the company's most popular and numerous type built. This example was built at the tail end of the Second World War in 1945. It was noted at Joe Nemeth Engineering in Easter Compton, just south of Bristol, during their public open day held on 2 October 2010.

Following on from the previous image, the next model produced by the company, in the form of the more heavy-duty Hanibal. This example built in 1956, was seen on 5 September 2010 while taking part in the Great Dorset Steam Fair.

This example was built in 1959 as an Industrial model, and was used by the RAF until 1966, when it was transferred to the ownership of BAA based at Heathrow Airport, where it remained until the mid-1990s, when it was purchased and placed in a container until 2010. It was pictured on 12 November 2011 at an auction in Redhill, Surrey.

18. Tippers and Dumpers

These vehicles are most likely to be found within the workings and confines of stone quarries, but they are not used exclusively for that purpose as such. These vehicles are heavy and extremely sturdy due to the nature of the workload they are designed to undertake.

Heinz, Pierce & Munschauer emerged in Buffalo, New York, in 1865. They manufactured household items, particularly delicate gilded birdcages. In 1872 George Pierce bought out the other two partners and renamed the company George N. Pierce Company, and by 1903 they began making automobiles (namely The Arrow). A year later the company launched its most successful car, The Great Arrow, and became the Pierce Motor Company. Due to the success of these cars, in 1908 the company was renamed in honour of the Pierce-Arrow Motor Car Company. That year also saw the beginning of the manufacturing of commercial vehicles; the company would also add fire engines, boats, camp trailers, motorcycles and bicycles to their repertoire.

Noted on Brighton Road in Purley on 1 May 2016 while taking part in the HCVS London to Brighton Run, this is a 1911-built Model 'R' tipper truck.

Pictured during the 'Steam on the Levels' event on 15 May 2016 at the Westonzoyland Steam Pumping Engine on the Somerset levels, this is a 1949-built Dennis Pax Elite MS LN1516 tipper. It was originally used by the Somerset County Council Highways Department.

Founded in Pittsburgh, Pennsylvania, as the Pittsburgh Motor Vehicle Company in 1897, they changed their name two years later when they moved to Ardmore, near Philadelphia, to the Autocar Company. They produced cars under the Autocar marque but in 1907 they decided to concentrate on commercial vehicle production. The last cars were made in 1911. The company remained in business until 1953 when they were taken over by the White Motor Company.

This dump truck was built in 1917 as a model UF21 for use by the American army. It was pictured in Stockland, Devon, on 24 August 2014, while on display at the Honiton Hill Rally.

In 1909 Benjamin Gotfredson (a horse seller) realised that the increase in automobiles on the roads would mean that trimming, painting and other accessories would become needed, and so he formed the American Auto Trimming Company, in Ontario, Canada, which became the largest paint and trim company in North America during the 1920s. Just after the First World War the company required more trucks to transport their products to and from the Ford Factory in Toronto. However, because of the war and having to pay import taxes from America, purchasing new trucks was expensive.

Gotfredson decided to build a few of the company's own trucks, so in 1920 the first trucks were produced bearing the G&J names (after Gotfredson & Frank Joyce – joint company heads). The venture proved highly successful and the company became the Gotfredson & Joyce Corporation Ltd. In 1923 they moved into full-time commercial vehicle manufacturing and rebranded themselves as The Gotfredson Truck Corporation and they would continue making trucks until 1948.

This 4-ton Series 80 model tipper was built by the company in 1923 and the retail price would have been $3,975. It was purchased in 2014 and imported for eventual restoration. It was seen at the Statfold Barn Railway Enthusiasts Day on 13 September of that year.

Willys Overland Crossley Ltd built this 2-ton tipper in 1930 under the Manchester brand marque. It was photographed at the premises of an agricultural engineering company in Mirfield, West Yorkshire, on 17 October 2015.

Built by Morris-Commercial in 1932, this type C11/40 tipper was seen at the Bridgwater Classic & Vintage Vehicle Show on 8 August 2015.

19. Wreckers, Tow Trucks and Recovery Vehicles

An essential part of the commercial vehicles umbrella, these vehicles are always seen on motorways parked up when road maintenance works are been carried out. They are also helpful if the vehicle somebody is travelling in breaks down and requires rescuing, be it in a car, coach/bus or lorry. The vehicles in this category range from basic 'beavertail' drive on ramp lorries up to the heavy-duty tow trucks and wreckers.

Part of the Teddy Tucker Collection that was auctioned in Taunton on 17 February 1990 was this 1937 tow truck built by Foden. It was pictured on the day of the auction, being closely inspected by a possible bidder.

Seen at Tarrant Hinton during the Great Dorset Steam Fair on 3 September 2010, this Foden DG6/S20 heavy-duty wrecker recovery vehicle was built in 1946.

This heavy-duty wrecker, seen on 29 April 2017 at the Abbey Hill Steam Rally, was built in Basingstoke by Thornycroft in 1949 as a Beg Ben, exclusively for use by the British Army, prior to being preserved.

The HCVS Annual London to Brighton Run is a very popular and well supported event, with a variety of commercial vehicles taking part. This 1959-built Dennis Pax Breakdown recovery truck is in the 1 May 2016 run.

Built in 1956 as a WD66N by Albion Motors, this wrecker recovery was taking part in the 2017 Abbey Hill Steam Rally in Yeovil on 29 April.

One of the many heavy-duty towing vehicles that were used over the years by the Billy Smart's Travelling Circus, this 1943-built Mack NM/NR 6x6 was seen on display outside of the now closed Bentley Motor Museum in East Sussex on 3 August 2013. Note that the vehicle is missing its bulldog motif from the bonnet.

Bolton, Lancashire, is where, in 1899, brothers Thomas and Joseph Hampson built an experimental motor car. In 1902 they had moved 34 miles west to Southport, where they founded Vulcan Motor Manufacturing and Trading and began producing low-cost, high-quality cars under the Vulcan marque. The company changed name in 1906 to Vulcan Motor and Engineering, continuing to produce automobiles until 1928. Just before the First World War they began manufacturing commercial vehicles and would continue to do so until 1953, when they were acquired by the Rootes Group.

This 6PF 'beavertail' recovery vehicle was built by the company in 1949 and was on display on 29 August 2011 at the Onslow Park Steam Rally in Shrewsbury.

This is a 1929-built Ford Model AA tow truck, seen on Brighton Road, Purley, on 1 May 2016 during the HCVS London to Brighton Run. It would easily be able to recover a Ford Model T or equivalent sized car if it broke down, however it would struggle to get the behemoth sized lorry (by comparison) that was following it an inch off the ground.

'Two for the price of one' on 5 September 2010 at the Great Dorset Steam Fair. This 1958-built Ford type D1210 'beavertail' recovery carries a 1956 Thames Trader dropsided vehicle on its back.

This interesting looking 'beavertail' vehicle has had a chequered history. It was built by Leyland in 1953 as one of two prototypes built on a defunct Leyland Tiger bus chassis. Following the abandonment of the project it was purchased by Clayton-Dewandre of Lincoln and was used by them as a heavy breaking systems test bed. Then the Lincolnshire Road Car Company acquired it for bus recovery work. It was sold to a private owner in 1992. Now fully restored, it takes part in many shows/rallies etc. On 12 September 2015 it was at the Statfold Barn Enthusiasts Day, soaking up the sunshine. It is believed that the other prototype was scrapped, thus making this example an extremely rare survivor.

In 1959 Austin built this lightweight Series III tow truck for use by the British Army. Noted on 5 September 2010 at the Great Dorset Steam Fair, minus its canvas overall cover, it has an almost skeletal-like appearance.

This type 981 was built in 1945 by the Diamond 'T' Company and originally used by the American Military as a tank transporter towing vehicle. It was later converted to a heavy-duty wrecker recovery vehicle, before being purchased by a private owner. It was seen on 18 July 2015 at Haverthwaite inside the museum of the Lakeside & Haverthwaite Railway in Cumbria.

Built as a 1943 Matador 0853 Artillery Gun tractor by AEC, before being acquired by the Lancashire United Bus Company and converted to a heavy-duty wrecker for use in the recovery of the company's fleet of buses, it is unique in that the covered area also acts as a staff mess room and tool store. It is pictured at the Greater Manchester Museum of Transport on 26 January 2013.

20. Miscellaneous Vehicles

In this final chapter I shall be looking at those vehicles that were either originally built as other vehicles that have been converted into commercial ones (cars for example) or those that have been purpose-built for a specific use not covered in the other chapters.

In 1930 Vauxhall Motors introduced the Cadet VY luxury saloon onto the market and produced them until 1933, manufacturing some 9,631. During the last year of production, they decided to build the cadet with a small goods van body in place of the saloon body. It is uncertain how many of these vehicles were built, but they were very few as they proved to be not popular with the public. This surviving example was seen at Winkleigh in Devon at the 7 October 2013 West of England Transport Collection open day.

In October 1895 British cycle designer and entrepreneur Harry Lawson founded the British Motor Syndicate (BMS), which had members of the public raising funds to acquire as many patents from manufacturers of automobiles as possible – then charge them an extortionate fee if they wished to build any of those patents. In November 1895 they purchased the Daimler Motor Syndicate Ltd – a shrewd piece of business that saw the shareholders of BMS make a profit of 200 per cent on their original investment in a month.

In January of 1896 Lawson launched a new company The Daimler Motor Company Limited in Coventry. They were an independent manufacturer until 1910 when acquired by the Birmingham Small Arms Company (BSA), the first of numerous different owners currently owned by Jaguar Land Rover.

Following the First World War, companies looked at new ways to advertise their products. Worthingtons was one and they commissioned Daimler to build five lorries in the shape of a beer bottle (each one depicting a different product). Built in 1924 on a TL30 chassis, this example was seen on 21 December 2013 at the National Motor Museum in Beaulieu. Note next to it is another promotional vehicle in the form of a Jaffa Outspan Orange car (one of six built by Brian Waite Enterprises on mini chassis).

Seen on 11 August 2012 at Bruton, near Frome in Somerset, during the Gilcombe Festival of Transport, this 1938-built Fordson 7V Luton van has been converted to transport the owner's stock car to/from various racing circuits (the rear of which is just visible on the left).

Founded in Manchester in 1904 by pioneer aviator Charles Rolls and engineer Henry Royce as Rolls-Royce Ltd, the company would become one the biggest and most well-known companies worldwide in luxury automobiles and engine manufacturing. Even with the death of Rolls in an air crash during an air display at Bournemouth in 1910, the company went on undeterred boasting that they made 'The Best Car In The World'. Like many other companies, they've had their ups and downs and numerous ownership/name changes, and the original company was finally wound up in 1971.

Although this wasn't the end of their story, a new government-owned company Rolls-Royce (1971) Ltd acquired the business and naming rights (the (1971) part of the name was dropped in 1977). Today the company is a subsidiary of Rolls-Royce Holdings Plc.

The company are not known as commercial vehicle manufacturers, but during the recession years of the 1920s/30s some of their 20/25 type saloons were converted by individuals or companies for this purpose. Built in 1923, this example was converted in 1939 for use as a military ambulance, using lightweight 'Kelvinator' heavy-duty aluminium for the bodywork. In 1950 it was purchased by an Australian couple who converted it into a mobile caravan for touring around the world. It was in that guise that it was pictured on 6 September 2015 while the couple were visiting the Haynes International Motor Museum in Sparkford.

Seen on 29 April 2017 at the Abbey Hill Steam Rally, this 1932-built 20/25 saloon had been converted during the 1940s to a 'dog-cart' pick-up, so called because they were popular with shooting parties on private estates to transport the dogs to and from the shoot. Some purists say this is an abomination to the Rolls-Royce name; personally I call it practical.

Built in 1935, this 20/25 saloon was converted to an estate car for big game hunting in Rhodesia. The bumpers were fitted with pole holders, so that an awning could be placed over the entire vehicle when parked in the African sun. The front seats had gun holders underneath them and the drop down windows would allow the participants to shoot from inside the car. This feature was used proficiently on occasions during the Second World War, when the car was captured by the Germans and used as a staff car. It was purchased after the war by the Wrigley family (of the chewing gum fame) and taken to their private California estate. In 2004 it was acquired and repatriated by the Lartington family, who run and own Charles Dickens' favourite restaurant (Rules, Covent Garden, founded in 1798), where it can often be seen outside advertising the restaurant in its current Tea & Sympathy Van guise. It was pictured going along Brighton Road, Purley in Surrey on 1 November 2015.

The CCKW353 was a long wheelbase vehicle built primarily for the US Army by GMC as a general purpose vehicle. This example was built in 1942 and was used by the military until acquired and bought to the UK in 1969, where its owner completely stripped it down and rebuilt it as a lime spreader for use in agriculture. It was on display at the Great Dorset Steam Fair on 5 September 2010.

In 1941 Chevrolet introduced the COE (Cab Over Engine) to their truck range, which were basically the popular AK series restyled. This example is an OJ version. It was built in 1946 and carries Mobiloil Vacuum Oil Company decals and is fitted with a Trailmobile insulated body. It was seen on 24 September 2017 at the Hampton & Kempton Waterworks Railway.